HIGH SEAS
SECURITY

FRANK CAMPER

Loompanics Unlimited
Port Townsend, Washington

High Seas Security
© 1993 by Frank Camper

Illustrations by Frank Camper

Published by:
Loompanics Unlimited
PO Box 1197
Port Townsend, WA 98368
Loompanics Unlimited is a division of Loompanics Enterprises, Inc.

ISBN 1-55950-102-2
Library of Congress Catalog Card Number 93-77150

Contents

SPECIAL NOTE

This guide book is about advanced security techniques, not about seamanship, use of normal shipboard radios, radio direction finding equipment, radar, computer navigation gear, or even elementary first aid and lifeboat survival. Other books, manuals, and video tapes cover these fundamentals. To get the most from this book, it is presumed you, as master or crew member of a seagoing vessel, already know these basics.

Introduction
Fighting Terror At Sea

There *are* pirates out there.

Most of us still think of them in the past tense, as romantic figures raiding the high seas for gold, glory, and adventure. The truth is that pirates were all thieves and most were cowards. They usually hit defenseless vessels close to shore and often slaughtered the crews to conceal their acts of robbery and murder.

Nothing has changed.

Today, *now*, as you read this, pirates lay in wait among the islands and coastlines, watching for pleasure boats with innocent passengers. They strike fast, catching their prey by surprise. When they board, they kill and steal, weighting and sinking the bodies of the weekend sailors and their guests and taking the boat itself as the prize.

Organized crime pirates prowl the fishing lanes and attack shrimpers and net fishermen, killing the crews, plundering the boats, taking the catch, and in some cases scuttling the vessels and leaving them to be discovered crewless and awash far from the fishing lanes.

Drug dealers always need boats to use for one-time runs. Some pirates make careers out of stealing vessels just to sell to the drug cartels.

As if pirates themselves were not enough, we have the threat of terrorists and revolutionaries who capture boats to use for their raids and missions, or attack business and cruise ships to make a political protest or statement. They don't care who gets hurt in the process. Terrorists are just pirates by another name.

Most losses to pirates are outside the U.S. "customs" waters, which is only 12 miles offshore. Fishing rights extend 200 miles out, one reason there is sometimes confusion as to what limit is what, but the Coast Guard can respond to any U.S. registry vessel in trouble *anywhere in the world,* as long as the vessel is not in the territorial waters of another nation.

"The pirates are out there," a 7th District Coast Guard officer in Florida said. "There's no doubt about that. When they take a boat it just disappears. We list it as missing and let the insurance companies handle it. We've never responded to a distress call from a boat that was being attacked because we've never had one. An unwritten law of seamanship is that you stop and help another vessel in trouble. We think most of the pirating is done by a small boat faking trouble, looking harmless, and when the yacht comes to her aid — bang, it's all over. They don't have a chance to call for help."

The most vulnerable target of the pirate is the small boat alone, such as the schooner or the sailing ship. Usually there are only two people aboard. Pirates don't want to deal with a lot of people, but sometimes even the bigger yachts go missing, with six or eight people aboard.

Onshore law enforcement agencies can't handle piracy. They might patrol the shoreline of their jurisdiction in small boats, but have no authority or capability past that. The usual reaction of coastal state police to an inquiry about piracy is "to let the Coast Guard handle it."

The modern pirate enjoys the same advantage now as his predecessors did two hundred years ago. At sea, might makes right. There are no police stations, no place for an attacked craft to run. The hard truth is, the best defense against pirates is common sense caution, knowledgeable deterrent tactics, and the preparation and will to use force if necessary.

Chapter One

How The Government Special Operations Units Do It

It can happen to you and your friends or family.

You might be in charge of or going on a yacht charter, or working on a fishing boat, or just out for a weekend's sailing in the islands, and suddenly armed men are coming aboard, taking over.

Who would come to save you and how would they do it?

The United States military has several units with the technical *capability* of fighting terrorism at sea, such as when a U.S. registry vessel or U.S. citizens on a foreign vessel are attacked or held hostage. These units do not always have that *mission,* because for legal reasons, most piracy or hostage situations at sea are considered civil police and not military matters. The U.S. Coast Guard is under the Department of Transportation, not the Pentagon, and therefore is considered a civil agency.

Before a rescue from pirates or terrorists by a U.S. military or civil unit can be launched, government bureaucrats with their own political priorities must first decide who is going to do it. The U.S. military does not have arrest powers. Obviously this is an awkward situation while the lives of you and others on your vessel are at risk, and all the more reason to prepare yourself and your own vessel to be as self sufficient as possible.

There is the Federal Bureau of Investigation's Hostage Rescue Team (HRT) which has rescue as its mission even at sea, where we also have the overlapping jurisdictions of the U.S. Navy and the Coast Guard.

The Navy has its SEAL (SEa Air & Land) teams, a unit of which *is* assigned to counterterror operations. The Coast Guard does not have SEAL teams, but it does have navy-trained SCUBA (Self Contained Underwater Breathing Apparatus) divers, and in the 1980s, undertook special counterterror and rescue training of its own, for its *LEDET* (Law Enforcement Detachment) teams.

The good news is the U.S. Coast Guard (USCG) can now work closely with the Navy or FBI teams for some types of counterterror operations. The bad news is it still takes time to decide who's in charge, whether it's a Navy op (operation) assisted by the Coast Guard and FBI or an FBI and Coast Guard op assisted by the Navy.

Let's take a look at some of the joint FBI/USCG training and operational hostage rescue techniques.

Hostage Rescue Training Objectives:

1. To create a capable team equipped and trained to isolate, investigate, board, and take control of a vessel docked, anchored, or at sea, preserving the life of hostages being held aboard by hostile individuals, and to take those individuals into custody.
2. To establish a working format and operating procedure between the USCG Law Enforcement Detachment team and any other cooperating intelligence, law enforcement, or military agencies.

3.   To deter future terrorism or criminal activities by the example of the efficiency of the combined services operations.

Complications

Obviously there are complications for seaborne tactical law enforcement operations against a hostile opposition, as compared to
those on land. Here are the main ones.
1.   There is usually little or no concealment for maneuvering of
the Boarding Party toward a Target Vessel.
2.   There is usually no cover to protect the Boarding Party from
incoming fire.
3.   The Target Vessel can escape, unlike a building on shore.
4.   The Target Vessel can be sunk, with loss of life of hostages,
Boarding Party personnel, and destruction or loss of legal
evidence.
5.   Limited space aboard a vessel hampers Boarding Party
movements during boarding and rescue operations.
6.   Lightweight construction of hulls and superstructures of
most pleasure craft increases the hazard of small arms fire
penetration and the transit of bullets which could accidentally strike hostages or Boarding Party personnel.
7.   Circular field of view from Target Vessel and observation by
suspects makes close placement of intelligence gathering and
other devices difficult prior to a rescue attempt.

The Rescuers

1. Command & Control Team
2. Support Team
3. Swim Team
4. Boarding Party
The COMMAND & CONTROL (C&C) TEAM consists of the
commanding officer, who may be military or civil, and is in charge
of all aspects of the operation, the officers in charge of each separate team, and all necessary assistants. The C&C Team works
through the Support Team.

The SUPPORT TEAM may be military or civil, and provides intelligence gathering, procurement of special equipment, air and surface unit coordination, liaison with other civil or military units, and sniper or *suppressive* fire (fire intended to overwhelm hostile fire).

The SWIM TEAM, for civil operations, may be specially trained Coast Guard or FBI personnel if it is expected that they must board to make arrests. Otherwise, a SEAL team is best qualified for this. The Swim Team delivers and places special equipment near or on the Target Vessel in preparation for the Boarding Party.

The BOARDING PARTY has the responsibility of boarding the Target Vessel, subduing the suspects, and removing hostages and prisoners from the vessel. For civil operations, the Boarding Party is usually the Coast Guard Law Enforcement Detachment team, because it is the USCG, not the Navy, which has arrest powers. Because of the complexity of civil agency influences (such as hostage negotiation, an FBI specialty) the boarding and arresting responsibilities might also include the FBI Hostage Rescue Team.

Qualifications And Training Of Boarding Party Personnel

Boarding a vessel with terrorists or pirates aboard who may violently resist is extremely dangerous and requires that the personnel who must board know:
- Small Boat Handling and Boarding Party Drill
- Deck Clearing Combat Techniques
- Power Tool Entry of Hatch, Door, & Hull/Superstructure
- Delivery of Small Arms Fire from Vessel Underway
- Disabling Vessels with Small Arms Fire
- Close Quarters Hand-to-Hand Combat
- Knife Attack & Defense
- Stun, Smoke, & CS (tear gas) Grenade Use Aboard a Vessel
- Pistol, Shotgun, & Submachine Gun Use Aboard a Vessel
- Basic Explosive Ordnance & Demolitions (EOD)
- Arrest and Prisoner Handling Methods
- Emergency Gunshot & Burn Injury Treatment
- Fuel & Fire Hazard Control Aboard a Vessel

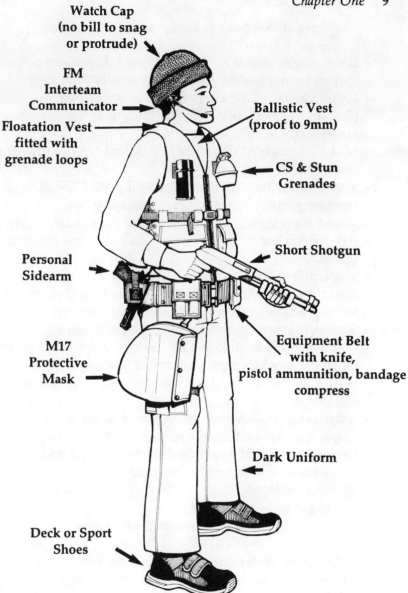

Watch Cap
(no bill to snag
or protrude)

**FM
Interteam
Communicator**

Floatation Vest
fitted with
grenade loops

Ballistic Vest
(proof to 9mm)

**CS & Stun
Grenades**

**Personal
Sidearm**

Short Shotgun

**Equipment Belt
with knife,
pistol ammunition, bandage
compress**

**M17
Protective
Mask**

Dark Uniform

**Deck or Sport
Shoes**

Figure 1-1
Boarding Party Member

Special Weapons & Equipment: Support Team

- LAW (Light Antitank Weapon) and Viper armor-piercing rockets for use against steel-hulled vessels.
- 40mm Grenade Launchers for firing armor piercing, high explosive fragmentation, smoke, and tear gas grenades, at ranges of up to 350 meters.
- M14 (7.62mm NATO) and M16 (5.56mm NATO) rifles for offshore or boat-to-boat fire.
- M60 (7.62mm) medium and Browning M2 (.50 caliber) heavy machine guns for disabling or suppressive fire.
- Sound suppressed, telescope-sighted 9mm submachine guns (HK MP5 SD or Sterling Patchett) for sniper use at 100 meters or less.
- Sniper rifles, 7.62mm and .50 caliber.
- Night vision sights (thermal & infrared/light amplification) for all machine guns and shoulder-fired weapons.
- Smoke mortar (launches floating smoke bombs).
- Radio-controlled detonation devices for disabling mines, other emplaced charges, and smoke dischargers.
- Long range directional microphone listening and recording equipment.
- Video and still-camera surveillance equipment with telescopic and night vision lenses.
- Underwater sound detection devices: receivers and monitors.
- Proper radio equipment for communication with all units and agencies involved.

Special Equipment: Swim Team

- SCUBA gear with rebreather (no bubbles) equipment.
- Underwater diver-to-diver voice communicator (CLASSIFIED).
- Underwater navigating wrist compasses.
- Spear guns and combat knives.

- Submersible, shielded illumination lamps for emplacing sound detection devices or doing other work at depth or in poor light.
- Buoyed rolls of steel cable for propeller/rudder fouling.
- Inflatable boat, weighted and deployable from below the surface.

Special Weapons & Equipment: Boarding Party

- Inflatable boats, six to eight person capacity.
- Boarding nets, lines, and hooks.
- Uniforms and caps, fire resistant.
- Deck or athletic shoes.
- Body armor appropriate to anticipated threat level.
- Flotation vests.
- Headset radios (for interteam and C&C communications).
- Halon fire extinguishers, small, for personal protection.
- Flashbang stun grenades.
- Aerosol type (nonflammable) CS tear gas grenades.
- M17 type protective (gas) masks.
- Shotguns with slugs and light and heavy shot (No. 4 & 00 Buck).
- Pistols.
- Gunshot wound bandage compresses and tourniquets.
- Handcuffs.
- EOD kit with lock and hinge cutting charges for team explosives ordnance specialist.
- Insulated-handle power tools and protective goggles for cutting into light metal, Fiberglas, or wooden-hulled vessels.
- Flare gun (for visual signals).

The "Q" Ship

The term "Q" ship refers to innocent-looking freighters used by the Germans during World War I, which were fitted with hidden guns and powerful engines. The "Q" ships flew false flags to fool the enemy, and once close to a vulnerable merchantman, would drop the canvas and wood superstructure panels concealing its guns, run up its true colors, and attack.

When the use of a marked, identifiable Navy or Coast Guard vessel for counterterror missions is not practical, the U.S. Navy has available a few of its own "Q" ships, which are a variety of modified civilian craft which resemble sport fishing boats or pleasure craft.

Figure 1-2
"Q" Ship

For counterterror operations, the Navy can provide these "Q" ships from its clandestine units which support SEAL missions. Sometimes the Coast Guard has these vessels on loan from the Navy, usually working in support of the Drug Enforcement agency (DEA), or the U.S. Customs Service.

In a hostage rescue scenario, a "Q" ship can act as a floating headquarters for the Command & Control Team and Support Team. To do this, the "Q" ship positions itself as close as possible to the Target Vessel, so surveillance and other intelligence gathering activities can be conducted without the knowledge of the suspects.

A reconnaissance "Q" ship is usually equipped with hidden camera ports, military radar and sonar, electronic eavesdropping gear for monitoring radio frequencies, electronic countermeasures (ECM) equipment to jam radio, radar, and sonar, and all the communications equipment necessary to provide sea, air, and land unit coordination.

Sniper, machine gun, grenade launcher, and LAW or Viper rocket fire can be delivered from a "Q" ship if necessary, and the vessel may be used to conceal or deploy a Boarding Party or swimmers.

For the crew's protection, a "Q" ship is usually fitted with unnoticeable bullet resistant materials (more about that later, in Chapter 2), and for desperate situations, some have reinforced bows for ramming.

Radio-Activated Smoke Discharger

Aside from rain or fog, smoke is about all the concealment a ship can get on the open expanse of the ocean. In wartime, smoke is used to obscure visibility to confuse downwind enemy gunners, who can't see which way the smokelaying ship is zig-zagging.

Smoke can be used in counterterror operations to blind gunners or lookouts on a Target Vessel, concealing the approach of a Boarding Party.

Most Navy and some of the larger Coast Guard ships have smoke generators aboard, and some vessels are equipped with smoke mortars which can fire large capacity smoke bombs designed to explode in the air or float and spew smoke, but firing smoke mortar bombs in a port or marina area where other vessels are docked or anchored may be too risky.

The problem with conventional smoke generators is they are mounted to the ship, and to cover an area in smoke, the ship must maneuver upwind of the target, something which may not be possible.

The answer is Swim Team emplacable, semi-submerged smoke dischargers which are individually activated by a radio signal.

Figure 1-3
Radio-Fired Smoke Discharger

These smoke dischargers are employed by swimmers, in groups surrounding the Target Vessel, to take advantage of whichever way the wind is blowing when it's time to provide smoke screening.

Both black and white smoke is available. Black smoke is usually for night operations, because it increases the darkness and conceals the fact smoke is present until it is covering the Target Vessel. White smoke is for daylight operations, because white has the best density for concealment in daylight.

Because the smoke dischargers are moored to the bottom via nylon lines, they are intended for shallow depths, typically harbors, ports, and marinas.

Disabling Mines and Sound Detection Devices

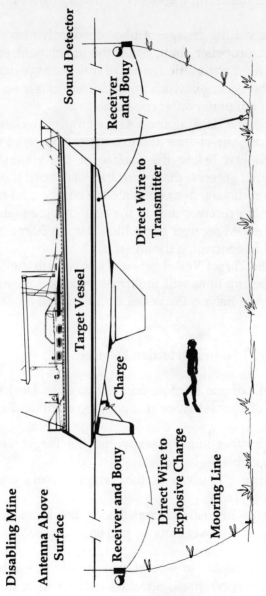

Figure 1-4
Disabling Mine & Sound Detector

If the decision is made to prevent the movement or escape of the Target Vessel, disabling the vessel by damaging its propellers or rudder is vital.

A ribbon-type cutting charge of plastic explosive may be applied around the propeller shaft, or on the attachment points of the rudder, and fired with little chance of hull damage due to the nature of the ribbon charge, which implodes and *cuts* metal with a minimum amount of underwater concussion.

The Disabling Mine (DM) unit consists of a prepared explosive charge; a reinforced, direct wire link to a battery powered receiver which is buoyed just below the surface of the water; a thin, camouflage-painted antenna that protrudes just above the surface for receiving the radio signal to detonate the charge; and mooring lines that secure the receiver unit to the bottom. Adequate line is provided with the DM receiver to position it up to 50 meters from the vessel, to aid in concealing the antenna.

In the event the Target Vessel gets underway with the DM unit attached, the mooring lines will pull free of the bottom so the receiver will be towed behind the vessel, and may still be detonated on command.

Sound Detection Devices

The attachment of one or more Sound Detection Device (SDD) units to the hull of a vessel gives the operation commander important information.
1.   Gunshots or other loud noises within the Target Vessel are readily detectable.
2.   Instant warning is given of the Target Vessel's engine attempting to start.
3.   Depending on acoustic circumstances, the location of personnel, and the movements of personnel aboard, is detectable.

SDD units are available in several configurations, but basically consist of a microphone that is attached to the hull of the Target Vessel, and resemble the Disabling Mine with a direct, reinforced wire link to a battery powered transmitter which is buoyed just below the surface of the water; an antenna which protrudes just above the surface for transmitting detected sound to a receiver station; and mooring lines that secure the transmitter unit to the bottom.

Also like the Disabling Mine, the Sound Detection Device will pull free of its mooring and be towed behind the Target Vessel if it gets underway, giving some hope to continue to monitor activities aboard the vessel once it stops again.

Rescue Tactics

The scenario we'll present here involves hostages being held aboard a commercial yacht anchored far offshore of a port or harbor facility. Of course, a rescue at sea would differ in some details from one in a harbor or port, but only in that an operation in international waters is more simple, because no state police agencies are involved, and less politics have to be practiced.

A more practical reason to present this scenario, rather than one farther at sea, is pirates holding hostages on a boat near a harbor is a situation more likely to be reported to the authorities. Like the 7th District Coast Guard officer said, small and medium sized craft at sea almost never have the opportunity to get off a radio call for help. So far, only the big ships such as passenger liners, once attacked or seized by terrorists, have been the subject of aid or rescue operations.

For military orderliness, rescues are generally divided into three phases:
1. ALERT
2. OPERATIONAL
3. ASSAULT

The Alert

The local Coast Guard station receives a call from the state harbor police; a robbery or piracy attempt on an occupied seagoing yacht anchored about a half mile out has been reported by another vessel, who attempted to help the yacht's passengers.

The pirates fired on the would-be rescuer, chasing him away, but he had made a call to the harbor police, who responded quickly. A police speedboat that approached the yacht was itself driven off by gunfire, but reports that the pirate's small boat has drifted away from the yacht, and the police boat is blocking the yacht's escape route to open sea. The pirates aboard the yacht realized they couldn't get away, and have radioed the police they have hostages aboard, and demand passage out.

The local FBI office, and all harbor police units in the area are notified by the police dispatcher of the situation as the nearest available USCG vessel arrives, and obtains identification on the Target Vessel registry and type, relaying a steady situation update to the Coast Guard station, which in turn is advising the District headquarters. A Law Enforcement Detachment Team Boarding Party is rapidly assembling at the local USCG station or district headquarters, anticipating the police request for assistance.

The LEDET team is transported (by helicopter, if necessary) to the harbor police dock, meeting the police tactical unit commander and the FBI's representative.

At this point, if the pirates have refused to surrender and are still demanding passage out, the local police, FBI, and Coast Guard command must decide whose operation it is going to be to rescue the hostages. A practical solution in a case such as this is to have the FBI carry out the hostage negotiations with the pirates, the state police to provide harbor security, keeping other vessels out of harm's way and continuing to block escape of the pirate's vessel or the Target Vessel, and the Coast Guard to go aboard if necessary and conduct the actual rescue.

As the police hand the hostage negotiations over to the FBI, the LEDET commander has the Target Vessel's deck plans and construction details faxed in from the dealer or boat manufacturer, and the team begins to study them to determine the best way to enter the cabins and compartments.

The hope is, as always, that the hostage negotiators can persuade the pirates to give up. Usually criminal suspects *will* surrender, but sometimes they don't. If the negotiating is going badly, and if the "suspects" aboard the Target Vessel are shooting at the police and Coast Guard to keep them from getting too close, the final option is to board, hostile fire or not.

If the police feel it necessary, they may try to evacuate civilians out of the harbor, to keep distant gawkers from being hit by stray bullets.

We're discussing common pirates here, not highly motivated, politically-backed terrorists. Terrorists rarely rob or hijack small civilian watercraft, but in the event they might, handling them has been anticipated by the LEDET. Handling terrorists is different, because terrorists' goals and tactics are different. Not to give too much away (some seaborne antiterrorist methods are classified), but if the terrorists refuse to negotiate, or are threatening to explode a bomb or do some similar damage, the FBI and LEDET might not waste time carrying out a dialogue intended only to stall, and just gather enough information to raid the Target Vessel as soon as possible.

If a "Q" ship is near enough to assist with the rescue, when it arrives the Support Team boards it. The "Q" ship moves in as close to the Target Vessel as possible, playing out its role of civilian pleasure craft.

Intelligence gathering and preparation for the assault begins. Long range directional microphones, video and still cameras, and night vision devices from the "Q" ship are focused on the Target Vessel. The Swim Team deploys from a suitable vessel to place smoke dischargers, underwater sound sensors, disabling mines, and propeller/rudder fouling cables.

Helicopter and recovery boat units are put on standby.

In an assault, the helicopters will hover in observation positions above the Target Vessel to direct the Boarding Party, warning them of unseen threats, and watching for people going overboard. The recovery boats will move in on the heels of the assault to pick up wounded or exhausted swimmers, anyone overboard, and take the hostages, prisoners, and any injured personnel off the Target Vessel.

The Boarding Party is briefed by the operation commander on the anticipated assault plan, and the specific equipment to fit the plan is selected.

Exactly when the assault must begin is determined by any deadlines or threats to harm the hostages the pirates may have given, but the reason an assault plan is made as soon as possible is to have some organization ready in case the pirates *unexpectedly* start killing hostages.

The Operational Phase

Intelligence gathering and coordination between agencies is critical during this middle phase.

The operational commander, whether police, FBI, Navy, or Coast Guard, is concerned with saving the lives of the hostages and the rescue personnel involved, with soothing jurisdictional conflicts between the agencies involved *(who, in a group effort, gets the credit for a job well done, who gets the blame for a failure?)*, with dealing with the press, and state or federal politicians who may want to decide, for their own public images, if the assault should be delayed, advanced, or even carried out or not.

The Boarding Party is concerned with the number and identification of the hostages and pirates, the pirates' armament, where the hostages are held aboard the vessel and where the pirates are positioned, and the intent and capability of the pirates to possibly sink or destroy the vessel if they are attacked.

In this scenario, we have two hostages aboard a light-hulled power vessel able to sleep six, being held in the galley, by at least three pirates armed with pistols.

As the hour chosen for the assault nears, the Support Team updates the Boarding Party on the latest intelligence. All units remain in a high state of readiness on standby to go.

The Assault

Speed is vital to saving lives in a rescue. To give an idea of how fast a well coordinated operation can be, we'll clock this predawn rescue drill.

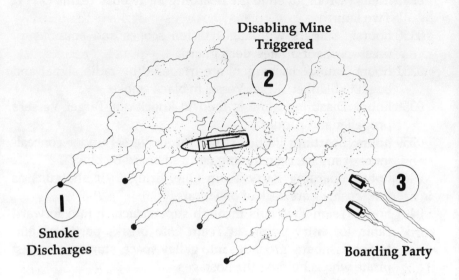

**Disabling Mine
Triggered**

2

1

**Smoke
Discharges**

3

Boarding Party

"Q" Ship **4**

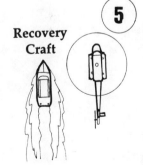

5

**Recovery
Craft**

Figure 1-5
The Assault

0345 hours: Order given to go. Boarding Party boat Teams One & Two launch.

0350 hours: Snipers with night vision scopes and sound suppressors shoot pirates' deck guard.

0351 hours: Smoke dischargers are triggered by radio signal and begin to blanket Target Vessel in black smoke.

0358 hours: Disabling mine is fired to knock out Target Vessel's propeller and rudder.

0359 hours: Boarding Parties reach Target Vessel under concealment of smoke, rig climbing net, and board by bow.

0400 hours: Boarding Party Team One, firing their shotguns as they rush, clears deck of one pirate.

0401 hours: Team Two cuts through superstructure into forward cabin for entry point, as Team One breaks portholes and tosses flashbang grenades into galley space, stunning the last pirate who is holding the hostages.

0404 hours: Hostages recovered by Team Two.

0405 hours: Boarding Party team leader reports hostages and vessel secured, and requests evacuation for wounded prisoners.

0410 hours: Support Team orders in recovery boats.

Chapter Two

Shipboard Security Equipment and Weapons

You read in Chapter One about all the gear the military and law enforcement agencies have. Let's divide what *you* need for your vessel into these groups:
1. Protective Materials & Equipment
2. Optics & Night Vision Devices
3. Radio & Signaling Equipment
4. Weapons
The use of this equipment is covered in Chapter Three.

Protective Materials and Equipment

These are bullet-*resistant* (nothing is really bullet proof) materials, electronic warning devices, and gas and fire masks.

Hull Armor and Ballistic Glazing

Because the hulls and superstructures of most pleasure boats are made of wood or fiberglass, they offer little or no protection against what the military sometimes calls a *ballistic environment*. That's milspeak for being shot at. The desirability of having a safe place to duck behind if someone starts blowing holes through your bulkheads needs no explaining.

Most small craft owners who use bullet resistant materials do so sparingly, just creating strategic places aboard to take cover behind, not trying to build battleships. What's best for your vessel configuration probably differs from another, but the typical mounting spots are side shields on the bridge and cockpit (to stand or crouch behind); low shielding on a deck (to lay down behind); and above-the-waterline shielding on fuel tank, cabin, hull, bulkhead, and hatches to make a temporary bunker if things really get bad. All exposed shielding is of course painted and decorated to look like a normal part of the vessel.

You could go to a welder and have 1/4" or 3/8" steel plates cut and fitted to protect your cabins, compartments, and engine bay, but the sheer weight of it is prohibitive for many small vessels, making some ride too deep and upsetting the trim and ballast balance on others.

Besides being heavy, steel is not necessarily guaranteed protection. *Mild* steel, so common for commercial construction applications, is actually rather soft and a quarter inch of it won't always stop a standard military full metal jacket rifle bullet. *Armor* plate, which is specially hardened (and therefore is a lot of work to bend and cut) is far better, but rare. The solution here is a compressed, laminated fiberglass and Kevlar fiber material used in shielding vehicles and buildings. Kevlar is a strong synthetic fiber used in body armor vests and some rigging lines and inflatable boat hulls. For vests, it is tightly woven and layered to meet different caliber threat levels.

At a mere one inch thickness, this composite material can *stop* most all high-powered commercial and military rifle bullets. It is lighter than steel for the same level of protection, doesn't rust, and is easier to cut and mount in place, requiring only the same bolts, screws and nails as wood. An advantage of this material is it "soaks up" hits, trapping the bullets within itself, where steel creates ricochets.

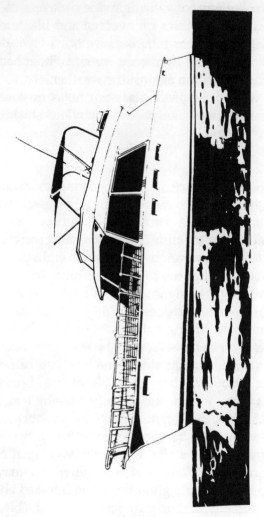

Figure 2-1

Properly installed, hull armor and ballistic glazing do not show.

Ballistic glazing, more commonly known by its more familiar, older misnomer, "bulletproof glass," is an excellent item for your vessel. The best glass can stop the same calibers as an inch of laminated fiberglass and Kevlar.

Most modern bulletproof glass is made of layers of glass and plastics, is about an inch thick on average and like laminated fiberglass and Kevlar, absorbs hits. Because of its layer design this glass is usually bulletproof from only *one side*. Fitted backwards it is little more than protection against the weather.

You would want bulletproof glass portholes in your shielded cabins, and it can serve as transparent, inobvious shielding panels for the bridge or cockpit.

Body Armor

A vest is good insurance if you're having to abandon your shielding and risk gunfire to move around the vessel. The average vest these days, a Type IIA Threat Level, is capable of stopping most pistol calibers up to 9mm Parabellum and some .357 magnums, and a IIA vest only weighs about six to eight pounds.

For marine use, an important aspect of some Kevlar vests' construction is how they may significantly *lose* bullet resistance when soaking wet, but sea water does not degrade the Kevlar, and it returns to normal after drying out.

Top-rated vests are expensive, and the vest you choose to wear in a ballistic environment should be the best you can afford. But for lesser duties, you can buy a couple of old, heavy, surplus military "flak" vests, which are actually intended to stop shell fragments, not bullets, but might manage to halt buckshot or a .38 special. These vests may be used to protect a wounded person from more harm, to cover a vital piece of navigational or communications equipment while bullets are flying, and may be most useful of all to throw atop a grenade or bomb tossed aboard, as it will stop a lot of fragments and dampen much of the blast.

The last thing to say here about vests is while they usually stop a bullet or fragment from entering your body, they don't stop you from suffering the impact, which could knock you overboard or knock you unconscious, or both.

Electronic Warning Devices

During the early morning hours while you're anchored in some tropical lagoon and everyone is asleep, pirates can be aboard before you know it.

What you need to foil this are some of the same basic kinds of detection equipment and alarms used in buildings. On land or sea the purpose is the same, to give yourself a few moments advantage against intruders.

These warning devices come in two types, permanently mounted and "portable" units. By portable, we mean transportable units that plug into onboard AC power outlets or are battery operated. Fixed units are specially wired into the vessel. The portables are obviously best for bare boat charters and the like, while your own vessel can use a combination of built-in units and portables.

Depending on the type of security system arrangement, you may have audible or "silent" alarms. Audible alarms are deterrents, intended to scare off intruders as well as alert you. Silent alarms give you an edge because they are *not heard* by the intruder, but alert *you* with a sound or light.

There are literally dozens of security devices available, so let's just examine what's practical for shipboard use.

Infrared Motion Detectors: These come in fixed and portable AC powered models. They work by sensing motion or body heat, and can trigger alarms or turn on lights.

Wireless Movement Detector: A portable unit. Battery powered motion detectors attach to hatches and doors and intrusion to a central AC powered receiver unit. The practicality of a unit like this aboard a rolling, pitching vessel may be limited because of the internal pendulum-type switches used in the standard electromechanical (vehicle alarm system type) motion sensors.

Hatch and Door Switches: This is a fixed, hardwired unit, available in DC and AC versions. Magnetic switches send an alarm signal when your hatches and doors are opened.

Pressure Sensitive Mats: Fixed and portable AC powered units. These mats, hardwired to an alarm system and hidden under carpet or other deck coverings, respond to footstep weight placed on them.

Photo Relay Sensors: Fixed and portable, hardwired and wireless, AC and battery units. Depending on the model, these project a light beam in the visible or infrared spectrum, and trip an alarm signal when the beam is broken. Some of these units operate as invisible tripwires, others as motion sensors when focused on a door, etc.

Vibration Detector: This is a personal, portable, battery powered unit with an audible alarm and is small enough to be carried in a shirt pocket. Vibration sensors are slightly different from automobile-type electromechanical motion sensors. A true vibration sensor is more high tech (no pendulum switch), and can be placed on a flat surface. Vibrations alone, without any visible movement, trigger this type of sensor.

Deciding on the types and placement of these devices depends on the size and layout of your vessel. Use your imagination when setting up or installing your warning devices. The portable infrared motion detectors are usually best aimed at deck areas where people are likely to try to board late at night. Optical sensors can create line-of-sight tripwires across decks. The alarm signal unit itself should be beside your own berth.

Gas and Fire Masks

Whatever type of "gas mask" (called *protective masks* by the military) you choose, the first thing you should know is it's foolish trying to use a gas mask in or near a fire, thinking you're safe from the smoke. Gas masks *don't* filter out the heat and carbon monoxide of a fire, and it doesn't take long inhaling such stuff for a human being to lose consciousness.

Firefighters wear special heavy duty "air pack" breathing equipment masks fed from large compressed air bottles worn on the back, but emergency, full-face air packs with small air bottles for shipboard use can be purchased from industrial and marine safety equipment suppliers, each mask unit in a sealed container, to be opened only when necessary.

Air packs are essential for fighting a fire on board, or for going below into a smoke-filled compartment to save a life. Pirates sometimes set a vessel afire to sink it or destroy the evidence of their plunder, and if you've survived a boarding but are left at sea on a burning vessel, an air pack might make it possible for you to live to go home again.

Now, back to gas masks. The types of gasses or chemical agents a mask can stop depends on the sort of filters in it. Tear gas, such as CN or CS (CS is more powerful, but both are effective) is actually *not* a true gas, being a cloud of particles so fine they float in the air. The basic filters used in virtually all military and police masks world wide are capable of stopping tear gas, and tear gas is really all we're concerned with, since pirates might try to force you off your vessel or from below decks with tear gas grenades, or vice versa.

A problem with gas masks is *salt or fresh water always reduces the effectiveness of the filters* and sometimes permanently ruins them. If you drop a mask overboard and recover it, change the filters.

Figure 2-2
U.S. M17-Series protective mask

You can buy good surplus German or Israeli (and soon, probably, ex-Soviet) masks and filters cheap. The excellent, expensive, U.S. M17 type masks sometimes show up in surplus shops, but be advised these are hardly ever legally surplused out, finding their way to the market via soldiers who steal and sell them to shopkeepers. If you find an M17 type, check to see that it's not cut or damaged and if it has its filters in place, because spare filters for them are hard for civilians to get.

Inspecting and testing *any* masks you buy (you should have at least two or more) is important. You don't want to be surprised by a missing filter, cracked eyepiece, or broken harness once a CS grenade bounces aboard from a passing speedboat.

Optics and Night Vision Devices

A lot of grief can be avoided if you see the bad guys before they see you.

Most boats have a knockabout set of common binoculars at hand, but that's not always good enough. At sea, you have corrosive salt water, widely varied light, rolling decks, and long visual distances to contend with, and overcoming these conditions requires special features. This section is about the best type of day and night vision optics for security purposes.

Binoculars

Binoculars are complex, involving lenses, prisms, and interior mirror/reflectors. This makes it possible to shorten the length of the tube holding the lenses, etc., unlike a telescope. The lenses of binoculars also cheat Mother Nature and "multiply" available light to make it easier to see after dark.

Any binoculars you take to sea should be rubber armored for protection and nitrogen filled to prevent internal fogging. You should carry at least two types of binoculars, one pair of "marine binoculars" and one pair of general purpose wide angle "field binoculars." Marine binoculars are usually heavy, well weatherproofed, and have large objective lenses and high magnification (8x56, for example) as compared to field binoculars.

By "field binoculars" we're referring to 7x35's or a similar designation. The U.S. military settled a long time ago on 7x35 as a good compromise combination of magnification and lens size. 7x35 allowed reasonably lightweight, compact construction, and good magnification, field of view, and light gathering capabilities.

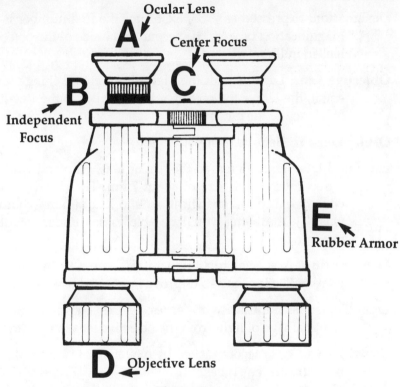

Figure 2-3
Understanding Binoculars

Binocular weight is important for two reasons. Lightness is an asset for long stretches of viewing, because after a while of constantly holding up a pair of binoculars, they begin to feel like an anchor, but heavy binoculars hold on target easier, an asset for stability with high magnification. The more powerful the binoculars, the jumpier the view. Every beat of your heart can shake the image. About 7x to 10x is the upper limit of practicality.

Binoculars

There's a lot of technical jargon used in describing binoculars. We don't need to get into all of it, but here's what you should know to buy what you need.

Designation: Expressed as 7x35, 8x56, etc., the first number is the magnification power. The second is the size of the objective lens in millimeters.

Objective Lens: Lens nearest the viewed object. All things being equal, the larger the objective lens, the better the low-light efficiency of the binoculars.

Ocular Lens: The lens nearest your eye.

Exit-Pupil Diameter: Refers to the ocular lens. Human eyes have a maximum pupil size of about 7mm. The closer the binocular's exit-pupil specification is to 7mm (more would be wasted), the better you'll be able to see under low-light conditions.

Lens Coating: A special treatment to the lenses to help reduce glare, reflection, and to improve light transmission.

Light Transmission: Clarity of lenses, prisms, etc., allowing efficient passage of light from the objective lens to your eye.

Center Focus: Focus accomplished by movement of a central knob between the lens tubes.

Independent Focus: Focus by separate adjustment of ocular lens turrets. Superior to center focus.

Field Of View: Maximum side to side area you can see when looking through your binoculars. Magnification alone tends to restrict the field of view, but this can be overcome in design. Binoculars with wider fields of view than average are called *wide angle*.

Night Vision Devices

As a U.S. citizen, you may legally buy and use virtually any type of infrared or starlight NVD, but you cannot sell or leave it outside of the United States. Night vision devices are covered under the U.S. Munitions Control Act and require special permission from the State Department to export.

NVDs vary greatly in design, price, and effectiveness. The least expensive are standard binoculars or telescopes which have lens coatings of *magnesium fluoride,* a substance that works with the light gathering ability of large objective lenses to enhance light transmission enough to allow you to see under low light conditions which uncoated lenses would not permit.

Next up on the price scale are infrared and "starlight" electronic light amplification equipment. By comparison with starlight, infrared is downright cheap. A good military surplus infrared spotlight and pair of detection goggles (armored vehicle crews wear these goggles to maneuver at night by infrared driving lights) can cost less than $500. The least costly *new* starlight scope is about $1000. Weapons sights in both technologies are considerably more expensive.

Infrared has one advantage over starlight, being that infrared works in *total* darkness, because it is projecting its own light source. Starlights work by taking available light, however dim, and electronically magnifying it thousands of times to create a visible image. At sea, moonless nights with heavy cloud cover can render starlight scopes almost useless.

The invention of starlight technology was hailed as a breakthrough because it had a *military* advantage over infrared. It used no light source of its own, therefore it was undetectable. Infrared light is invisible to the human eye, but it is *very visible* to another infrared scope. Starlight scopes are called "passive" night vision devices because they operate with no "active" projected light source. Infrared is considered an *active* NVD. Because you're not using infrared under battlefield conditions, its active designation is of little concern.

Each type of device, infrared and light amplification, has its good and bad points, which are usually examined in reference to land based infantry or commando operations. This time, we'll consider which is better for shipboard use.

Infrared is simply light normally invisible to us. Because it *is* light, it takes power to produce, and this is one of the usual gripes against it by troops in the field. For sustained use, infrared spot-lights need large automobile type batteries just like "white light" spotlights, and such batteries are heavy for troops to carry. Aboard ship you have your own power, and in the case of those very small craft that don't, you at least don't have to physically lug batteries around like an infantry soldier would.

Starlights do have the asset of requiring very little electricity, and one or two small flashlight or transistor type batteries can power them for many hours.

You don't see colors under infrared or starlight, the common view being variations of ghostly phosphor green because of the image optics design, but you do see all the reflections you'd expect under white light. Glossy hulls, superstructure trim and bright-work, foam atop wavelets, and glass portholes all glitter and gleam in the phosphor glow.

Starlight scopes can not only magnify available light, but also have sensitivity in the infrared spectrum. Infrared spotlights and lamps can be used to help illuminate an area or vessel. Because light amplification is usually not good enough at any distance to reveal the inside of a vessel through a porthole, throwing an infra-red beam inside gives you the same visual results as a white light spotlight would, because the infrared light reflects around inside the cabin.

For cost-conscious civilian security purposes, starlight scopes are better suited for weapons sights, but as general purpose view-ers they are convenient because their need for only a couple of small internal batteries gives them light weight and portability. Handheld starlight viewers usually have a pistol grip design and single-eye viewing.

The military uses different types of starlight goggles for vehicle drivers and helicopter pilots, and handheld or mounted scopes of various magnification powers and sensitivity for observation and surveillance. Goggles are the most expensive, but are the most useful aboard ship.

The newest, most sophisticated scopes can allow you to see clearly for hundreds of yards. You may have seen video tape shot through starlight optics, particularly the dramatic gun camera sequences recorded by U.S. aircraft in Iraq during the Gulf War. They represent the quality of resolution of the current generation of military NVDs.

Buying older starlight equipment is risky, because light amplification night vision devices use *image tubes* very much like television tubes, which create the electron images for your eyes. The tubes lose brightness after so many hours of use, and at some point have to be replaced. First and second generation starlight scopes typically had image tube lifetimes of two to four thousand hours. The newest equipment is much better, with ten-thousand-hour tubes.

Infrared equipment does not use these types of image tubes and no periodic replacement is necessary. The cost of a new light amplification image tube is usually about half the total cost of a new starlight scope, so the price of restoring an old starlight type scope to good condition can be substantial.

With the exception of specially waterproofed (and for civilians, unavailable) scopes used by SEAL teams, common infrared or starlight equipment is very vulnerable to shipboard hazards. You have to take the same care of it as you would your good camera equipment. For instance, although NVDs are reasonably sealed against moisture, salt sea air can cause corrosion in the battery compartments, so liberal swabbings of the battery contacts with WD-40 or a similar electrically conductive corrosion inhibitor is routine maintenance.

We'll discuss the practicality of night vision weapons sights for marine use later in this chapter.

Radio and Signaling Equipment

VHF Walkie Talkies:

In addition to your normal VHF shipboard radio, you should have at least *one marine-quality, handheld, battery powered VHF radio* kept with your survival equipment. This second radio doesn't just stay stowed. It goes ashore during island beach parties, or out with the dinghy in strange ports, in short, anytime there's a split up of your crew and passengers, so warnings can be radioed between them and the vessel. The reason for a portable VHF marine radio and *not* just a set of CB walkie talkies or other such available communications equipment, is your marine VHF radio links you quickly to channels 16 or 9 for security, mayday, and pan-pan calls.

Smoke Grenades:

Smoke markers are part of most lifeboat kits, but here we're referring to standard military type smoke grenades. They don't float and are not meant to be handheld while discharging, but they do create immense clouds of smoke which in most cases is more dense and persistent than lifeboat smoke markers, especially the military white smoke, which is excellent for smoke screens.

Flares:

Again, lifeboat stocks contain flares, but you should have a few of the military rocket-parachute and "star cluster" type because they usually go higher and are visible longer than the standard pen launcher and hand flares in survival kits. *Flare guns* or 12 gauge shotgun flares are also good, because they can be used offensively.

Tracer Ammunition:

Tracer, in the military calibers such as 7.62mm & 5.56 NATO, can substitute for flares when trying to signal rescuers. Just be sure not to make it look like you're shooting at them.

Weapons

For firearms, like night vision devices, a legal warning is necessary. Do not sell or leave firearms outside the United States, because it is a violation of U.S. federal law. The "exportation" of firearms (even just one) requires special Bureau of Alcohol, Tobacco, and Firearms (BATF) licensing *and* State Department permission.

The legalities of carrying firearms must be observed in U.S. as well as foreign ports. The U.S. government says any firearm that is legal on American soil is legal on an American vessel. The only hitch here would be the observance of state laws to insure a legal handgun in Florida does not get taken ashore in New York City, where it would be against the law.

If you take a firearm to a foreign port, and if the island or foreign nation in question gives permission in writing to a yacht or ship owner to have a weapon within their waters or to take it ashore, all the bases are covered.

But what if you don't have permission?

An American vessel docked in Bermuda, for example, is not going to be boarded and searched by the authorities without good reason. You have to be doing something wrong for them to want to come and search you. The port authorities know there are firearms on almost every vessel, and they don't care.

An obvious note about any firearms you may carry aboard is stainless steel is better for marine use, because of its corrosion resistance. At sea, even the best blued or parkerized metal is subject to daily rusting.

If you are carrying a blued steel firearm, the best rust preventative is military CLP (Cleaner/Lubricant/Preservative) or one of its commercial versions. CLP is good enough for SEAL teams to depend on, and serves alone to replace all other bore cleaners, oils, and greases in temperate and tropical climates.

Shotguns:

Probably the most versatile firearm available to pleasure boaters is the twelve gauge pump action shotgun.

First, shotguns don't have the same menacing appearance to customs inspectors or passengers as military type weapons do.

Secondly, there is a variety of specialty ammunition available for 12 gauge shotguns. In addition to the usual selection of steel and lead shot sizes, you can get hull-piercing slugs and signal flares. A slug is a single bore-size lead or steel projectile.

Figure 2-4
12-gauge pump shotgun:
probably the most versatile firearm available.

Some shotguns are called "slug guns" because they have rifled barrels and rifle sights. Different types of slugs are available, from the common ball for hunting, to high velocity pointed or hour-glass shapes police use for penetrating car bodies and blowing off house door hinges.

Last but not least, a shotgun's excellent shot-dispersion pattern also gives you a better chance of hitting a target from a heaving deck.

Pistols:

If your only firearm is a pistol, carry a large caliber, long barreled revolver. The larger calibers (.357 and .44 magnum) and long barrel (six to eight inches) give you range and penetration power. The simplicity and reliability of a revolver and its relative ease of cleaning as compared to an automatic, is well suited to shipboard use.

If you can, keep at least one more small pistol aboard, revolver or auto, as a hideaway gun stowed where pirates won't think to look for it. Being able to get to a backup pistol like this can be the deciding factor in your surviving a plunder or hostage situation.

**Long Barrel
.357 Magnum**

.45 Automatic

**9mm Browning
High Power**

Figure 2-5
*A pistol aboard could be the deciding factor
in your surviving a plunder or hostage situation.*

Rifles:

Semiautos and military calibers are best here. You're not carrying a rifle for hunting purposes, but for defense, and firepower is your primary concern. The caliber must be potent enough to pierce wooden or light metal hulls in case you must fire to hole or disable another vessel.

**7.62mm NATO
(.308 cal.)
M14 Rifle**

**FN-FAL
7.62mm NATO**

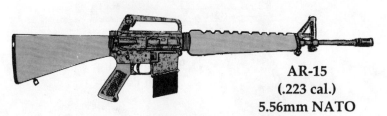

**AR-15
(.223 cal.)
5.56mm NATO**

Figure 2-6
*You're not carrying a rifle for hunting purposes,
but for defense, and firepower is your primary concern.*

We recommend military calibers because you can get armor piercing and tracer ammunition in them, something not usually available in civilian calibers such as .270, .30-30, etc.

7.62mm NATO or .30-06 armor piercing is capable of penetrating even heavy wooden hulls and doing severe damage to fuel tanks, engines, and other equipment inside. 5.56mm (.223) is a manstopper and can shred a fiberglass superstructure, but it can't always be depended on to punch a hull and damage an engine enough to put a boat out of action.

Submachine Guns:

As a rule, don't carry these. Subguns make a lot of scary noise, but it takes a pro to use what accuracy they have, and the pistol calibers they fire are no more effective than if they came from pistols.

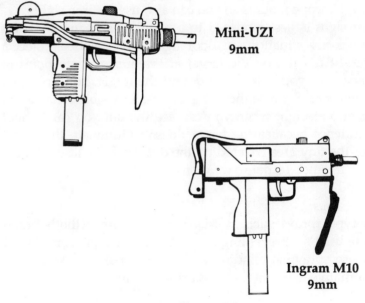

Mini-UZI
9mm

Ingram M10
9mm

Figure 2-7
As a rule, don't carry these.
You'll look like a drug dealer.

Even if you have BATF registration for the weapon, subguns excite everybody the wrong way. You'll look like a drug dealer with one, and losing one at sea will get you into felony trouble with BATF, because without proof positive of an accident they're not going to believe you.

Special Sights:

Starlight or infrared night vision weapons sights are good items, but for shipboard self defense you're generally better off with a more practical telescopic or laser sight, two types of sights which serve very different purposes.

A telescopic sight is best mounted to a rifle — not a pistol or shotgun — for long range shots. This is because telescopic sights severely restrict your field of view, and pistols and shotguns are quick-response, minimum accuracy weapons. The best scope for marine use is a 1.5x power, wide-angle type, fitted to the rifle with "see through" scope mounts so you can also use the iron sights.

A laser sight is best mounted to a pistol or shotgun for short range, quick-fire situations in poor light. Laser sights project a visible bright red dot on the target at the approximate point of bullet impact, so you look at the dot on the target, not through a sight, as you fire. Because the dot is not easily visible far away in daylight, and at night when you can see the dot you can't shoot with confidence because the beam doesn't illuminate the target except for the tiny area covered by the dot itself, the laser sight is best suited to quick-response weapons.

Tear Gas Sprays:

Police-type sprays such as Mace and Paralyzer (both brand names) are used for preventing hand-to-hand combat. A faceful of any of these sprays is blinding and terribly painful. As a close range alternative to gunfire, sprays are excellent.

Tear Gas Grenades:

CN and CS tear gas grenades are for using to clear pirates off your vessel *if* you have a mask, or for throwing aboard a pirate vessel to keep them busy while you break contact and get underway. Old style one-piece grenades will do, but the best are the newer types which break into several sections so they can't all be thrown back or overboard.

Improvised Incendiaries:

In extreme situations, you might have to destroy a hostile vessel by fire. The reason we're not suggesting explosives is because incendiaries are easier to make from available materials, and safer to use. The construction and use of improvised incendiaries is explained in Chapter Three.

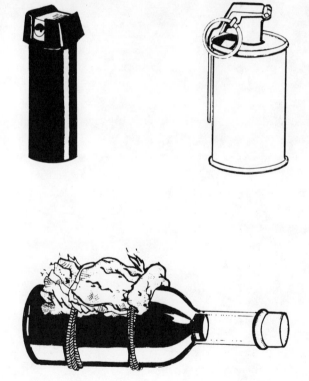

Figures 2-8, 2-9, and 2-10.
*Tear Gas Spray (2-8), Military CS Tear Gas Grenade (2-9),
and Improvised Incendiary (2-10).*

Chapter Three
Training

By training you're not trying to reach a warship-like level of proficiency or turn your weekends or voyages into paranoid military exercises. The purpose of training is to make your precautionary measures second nature, just like you prepare for storms or other nautical dangers.

Training is divided into:
1. Equipment Familiarization
2. Weapons Training
3. Emergency Drills
4. Daily Security Procedures

Equipment Familiarization

To increase your family's, crew's, passenger's, and your *own* chances for survival, you must truly know the many uses, capabilities, and limits of every piece of security equipment you take aboard.

The first step in being self-taught is to read the instruction booklet for each piece of equipment *in its entirety.*

The next step is to read and study tactical and technical manuals about the flaws, advantages, and clever uses of your equipment not always covered in instruction booklets.

Last, and the point of this section, is to take the equipment out to sea and put it through all its paces under varying conditions of light, darkness, and weather.

You can accomplish a lot by training with and testing your equipment on your regular excursions and voyages, but it will probably still be necessary to schedule special outings during bad weather and other conditions you may normally try to avoid.

Here are the kinds of questions you need to answer by experience, because in finding out, you will discover important things about yourself and your vessel as well:

- Do any peculiarities of your vessel's design, construction, or electrical system create inoperable or blind spots in your electronic warning device system?
- While wearing a body armor vest and/or protective mask can you do all the things necessary to control your vessel?
- Have you tested your protective mask or air pack in actual tear gas or smoke?
- Have you actually fired at least one of each type of flare, smoke, other signal pyrotechnic, or tear gas grenade you pack in your security equipment to observe its effects?
- Have you fired a signal flare in day and night rainstorms to compare its brightness to daylight or a clear night?
- Can you locate a small unlit vessel in heavy seas with your binoculars or night vision device, identify its type, and visually track it for at least an hour by day or night?

- How much does rain or fog reduce the range and clarity of your binoculars or night vision device?
- Can you operate your radio equipment blindfolded or one-handed?

Of course, these are just a few of many possible questions, but you get the idea.

Weapons Training

The three types of rifle ammunition you need are:

Ball

Tracer

Armor Piercing

Ball is the military term for full metal jacket (FMJ) bullets. These are lead bullets with brass jackets, and since both metals are relatively soft, ball ammo is a good but not a great penetrator, tending to mushroom and fragment, losing its velocity.

Tracer is a FMJ bullet specially marked with a red-painted tip, and it works via a small chemical charge embedded in the rear of the bullet itself. The charge is ignited by the heat of the powder in the cartridge case being fired. The charge burns as the bullet is in flight, leaving a visible streak of flame behind it. You can correct your fire by watching the tracers as they strike near your target.

Tracer ammunition can start fires if it lodges in the hull or superstructure of a target vessel before the tracer element has burned out. You can test this for yourself with piles of wood.

Armor Piercing (AP) in NATO military issue is usually marked with a black-painted bullet tip. AP ammo has the same powder load as a ball or tracer cartridge, but uses a hard *steel* bullet encased in a full brass jacket. The soft jacket engages the firearm's rifling and protects it from the bullet's steel core.

When firing AP, the closer you are to your target the better, because velocity of the bullet is critical to penetration, and velocity begins to diminish the instant the bullet leaves the muzzle. AP fired from a .308 (7.62mm NATO) rifle can at two to three hundred yards penetrate 3/8 inch to 1/2 inch of untempered steel plate. At three hundred yards, the .223 (5.56mm) SS109 AP fired from an AR-15A2 will reliably punch 1/8 to 1/4 inch. Earlier AR-15 and M16 rifles won't give you the same results because of a rifling difference. The A2 stabilizes its bullet better for armor piercing, but in doing so sacrifices wound trauma effects.

12 Gauge shotgun ammunition comes in two types, the standard 2 and 3/4-inch shell and the 3-inch magnum shell. When you buy your shotgun, it's best to get one that can use both. The most powerful shot size is 00 ("double ought") Buck, which is .32 caliber shot, meaning each pellet is .32 hundredths of an inch. "Buck" gets its name from *buckshot* used to kill deer. All other shot sizes are smaller and lighter and therefore have less range and do less damage. Lead 00 Buck can carry 100 yards with enough velocity to wound if not kill.

A shotgun shell only holds about a dozen 00 Buck pellets, and as such doesn't always fully cover a circular shot pattern, but enough Number 4 shot (1/4 inch or .25 caliber) pellets fit into a shell to provide a good pattern at 25 yards and less.

Lead is the traditional shot material, but steel shot is available. The military uses it because unjacketed lead shot or bullets are forbidden by the Geneva Convention, and duck hunters use steel shot for sporting and ecological reasons. Steel shot will penetrate superstructures and light hulls better than lead shot, but the lesser weight of steel shot reduces its inertia and likewise its range.

Now let's discuss using this ammo. There are three types of firing to anticipate:

1. *Long Range*, which might be necessary if you were under pursuit and wanted to scare off the chaser, or if you were trying to damage or stop an escaping pirate. This is what your rifle and a wide angle scope is for.
2. *Volume Fire*, against a raiding party or close, hostile vessel. For this you need a semiautomatic rifle or pump shotgun.
3. *Close Range*, to repel boarders, which is the specialty of the pistol and shotgun.

To get experience and improve your accuracy, your target practice must be done first from land, then from a stable vessel anchored or tied in calm waters, and finally from a vessel underway in different sea and weather conditions.

Target practice begins with standard sight-adjusting zeroing at paper targets at a firing range. Once you are hitting the bullseye with consistent accuracy and can quickly reload, clear malfunctions, and safely use all your firearms features and functions, you're ready to begin practical shooting.

To learn firsthand how your calibers affect hulls, super-structures, bulkheads, engine blocks, etc., find some old beached, abandoned vessels and spend an afternoon shooting them and examining the results. Under controlled conditions like this you can learn a lot.

Figure 3-1
Target Raft

Next, it's time to cast off. You should tow out an old raft to use as a target platform, to get used to shooting at small craft. Set oil drums on the raft, and on them tape target silhouettes so you can assess your hits.

Tie up the target raft to an old pier or buoy, and anchor yourself about 25 yards away in calm water. The object here is to *get hits*, not just make threatening splashes. You'll discover at once the difference between firing onshore and from a swaying deck. Even "calm" water, with its swells and currents creates movement, and hitting with any consistency takes acquiring the marksmanship equivalent of sea legs.

When you feel you're ready, tape up new silhouettes and tow the target platform out farther to choppy seas, load with tracer, and while underway, begin to shoot to *hit* the silhouettes, starting with 25 yards range and one target, gradually pulling in the towline to 15, 10, and 5 yards, shooting at different targets each time. After a few repetitions of this, you'll begin to get better, and appreciate tracer ammunition.

Finally, change all the silhouettes again and cast off the target platform. Sail away to at least 100 yards and begin your shooting from there, trying for hits on anything. The obvious problem, if you're out alone, is controlling your vessel and shooting at the same time. Working with a crew member is a bit easier. The gunner can give maneuvering commands to the helmsman, a training experience in itself, as you circle and close on the target platform.

Once the basic target practice learning is over, you should advance to shooting the same sequence again under different weather and light conditions, wearing your body armor vest and protective mask.

Hand-to-Hand Combat

This is the worst situation you could get into, and you must be prepared for it. It's outside the scope of this book to go into the details of hand-to-hand techniques, except for this one vital point:

When your life is at stake, never fight unarmed if there is anything you can pick up and use as a weapon.

In the event you are forced into hand-to-hand combat, there are no rules. Use knives, tools, oars, marlinspikes, *anything* you can grab to end it quickly.

There are many good manuals on hand-to-hand combat, and schools of instruction are plentiful. If you anticipate this kind of fighting, take the courses.

Using Tear Gas and Smoke

The typical gas grenade scenario is someone throwing one aboard your vessel or you throwing one aboard somebody else's. Either way you're close, and a shift of wind can bring your own gas right back to you.

Obviously, the wind is all-important if you're using gas or smoke. This is true even with tear gas sprays. People who spray into the wind to try and stop an attacker usually get the attacker *and* themselves.

If you get a strong dose of tear gas you will not be able to effectively defend yourself or your vessel. Whenever you're using tear gas spray or grenades, put on your mask first.

CS Tear Gas Effects

EYES	Burning sensation
	Heavy flow of tears
	Involuntary closing of eyes
SKIN	Stinging or burning sensation on moist areas
	Blistering of exposed skin from heavy concentrations
NOSE	Irritation-burning sensation
	Nasal discharge
MOUTH	Salivation
LUNGS	Irritation-burning sensation
	Coughing
	Tightness in chest
	Feeling of suffocation
	Panic
GASTROINTESTINAL	Nausea & vomiting
CENTRAL NERVOUS	Headache
SYSTEM	Dizziness
	Inability to take effective action
	Prostration up to several minutes for some people

Military type tear gas grenades have very short 9/10ths second fuse times. Once you pull the pin and release the safety handle, the fuse activates. Tear gas begins spewing almost instantly. Combat type CS grenades in metal canisters contain a fuel which is ignited by the grenade fuse. The fuel burns hotly enough to start fires aboard near flammable materials as it disperses the tear gas.

Because picking up a hot gas grenade (with a rag or glove) and throwing it back or overboard is easy for those on the receiving end, a grenade design exists which either separates a metal grenade body into several parts (each one busy spewing gas) or in the case of plastic grenades, completely fragments the body in a fire-cracker-like explosion.

An aerosol type gas grenade is also available, which will not start fires. This type is fitted with a locking spray nozzle instead of a fuse, and resembles an insecticide spray "bomb" of the sort used to fumigate a house.

If you are caught without your mask and are being gassed, there is some relief in soaking a shirt or towel with water (salt water is okay) and breathing through it. This won't allow you to see, but it's better than nothing.

Sweat makes tear gas work more efficiently and burn your skin more fiercely. You can *wash off* tear gas if you have lots of water, but be warned tear gas *spreads* in water like oil, and if you have tear gas contaminated water sloshing around on deck, the moment it splashes on you you're going to feel it.

Clothing contaminated with tear gas will continue to burn your eyes and skin and must be taken off and washed out over the side.

Military Smoke Grenades

These have metal canisters with the same 9/10th second fuse used in tear gas grenades. Like tear gas grenades, military smoke grenades also use a fuel that ignites a smoke chemical which can start fires on a wooden deck or near flammable materials. Some civilian smoke grenades are as dangerous as the military types because they have paper and plastic bodies which can burn away.

If you "pop smoke" on your deck, put the grenade in a metal pan or large open can to avoid igniting wood or cracking fiberglass.

Smoke grenades are primarily for signaling, but they may be used defensively or offensively. For defense, if a hostile vessel is shooting at you in a chase, you can pop a few grenades off your stern to create a smoke screen. For offense, you can throw a smoke grenade below deck into a hostile vessel's cabins or galley to blind and confuse anyone inside and drive them out.

In fact, a white smoke grenade popped on deck or below very convincingly simulates a burning vessel. You can fake a fire on your own vessel if it suits your needs, or by throwing a smoke grenade aboard another vessel, make its crew think they're afire.

Smoke grenade smoke isn't hot and is mainly just airborne particulate matter, and gas masks will filter out most of it, but remember, smoke from a genuine fire is loaded with heat and carbon monoxide.

Offensive Use Of Flares

The incendiary effects of a fiercely flaming rocket-propelled flare in spilled fuel or landing inside a galley or wood paneled cabin, and the impact wounds and burns one can inflict on people, make the signal flare a dangerous weapon indeed.

Survival kits usually contain pen type cartridge flare launchers, which work for very close point-and-shoot situations. These small flares are not lethal, but are extremely distracting if fired at someone's face or midsection. They don't penetrate into skin, but can easily blind an eye. Usually they impact and burn into the target's clothes, jetting torch-like flame. Be forewarned that if you fire one of these pen flares inside a cabin and it doesn't stick in an attacker's clothes, it sometimes tends to crazily ricochet around several times before burning out.

Flare pistols are familiar to mariners so little has to be said about them here, but other types of flare *firing* guns may need some explaining.

Probably the most familiar flare-firing gun is the 12-gauge shotgun. 12 gauge flares from a shotgun are surprisingly aimable at ranges up to 10 yards or more because of their ballistics, and have enough velocity to inflict serious injuries.

The 37mm signal flare has long been a military nautical standard because its large diameter allows a powerful rocket motor and generous payload. Small craft owners normally don't carry 37mm because of the size involved, opting for the smaller and easier to stow types.

Two examples of flare-firing guns chambered in 37mm are Smith & Wesson's single shot (tear gas) riot models and the MM1 Multi-Round Projectile Launcher. We mention these two launchers because in addition to firing 37mm flares and tear gas, they also launch smoke projectiles. Both of these are hard to find but they *are not illegal* for private ownership because they are smoothbore launchers and technically not firearms.

The single shot break-open Smith & Wesson guns resemble the U.S. M79 40mm grenade launcher. In fact, the army chose 40mm for its grenades so they could not be loaded into 37mm launchers.

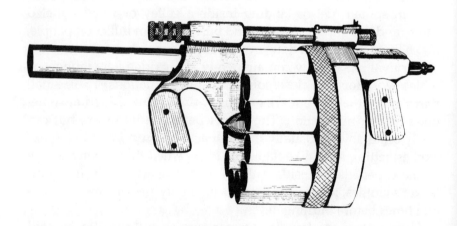

Figure 3-2
MM1 37mm tear gas, smoke, and flare launcher.

The 12-round rapid fire MM1 is a derivative of the 1930s era 25mm Manville Gun, a riot-breaker which fired tear and nausea gas. It may look familiar because real Manville Guns were used in the mercenary movie *The Dogs Of War*, but portrayed as if they were firing howitzer shells.

With either the S&W or the MM1, accurate fire can be placed on a hostile vessel, plunging incendiary flares, tear gas, and smoke aboard as fast as you can reload.

Improvised Incendiary Devices

A word of caution here... this information is included for a last ditch life-or-death situation. In addition to being extremely dangerous, incendiary devices are usually considered illegal under federal and state law.

The classic "Molotov Cocktail" is a seemingly simple device, being a gasoline filled glass bottle with a rag fuse stuck in the top. As simple as this sounds, a lot can go wrong. Lit fuses sometimes extinguish as the bottle is thrown, the bottles sometimes don't break when they hit the target, and worst of all, sometimes the bottles can accidentally break in your hand or gas can spill out on you past a fuse. If that happens and there's fire anywhere near, you're toast.

If you have to make a Molotov, fill the bottles with gas, and seal them with a cork or their original screw-on caps, and securely tape or tie a rag or paper fuse to the side of the bottle. Only prime the fuse with a flammable liquid when it's time to throw the Molotov.

For a longer lasting flammable than pure gasoline, you can take a fuel mixture from gas and diesel at about 50% gas to 50% diesel, or gas and motor oil, at 80% gas and 20% oil, because too much motor oil may make the mixture fail to ignite.

If a Molotov isn't right for the job, you may need the persistence of homemade napalm. Gasoline itself can burn out too fast, or run off hulls and decks into the sea. The advantage of napalm is because it's jelled it can stick to something while it burns. There is a very common misconception that the simple mixing of cold gas and "soap" powder or "soap" bar shavings automatically makes napalm. *It does not.* Neither do Molotovs explode. These misconceptions began with the simplistic and incomplete formulas once circulated in 1960s revolutionary literature, which later became popular misinformation among survivalist and paramilitary groups.

True soap is made from animal fat, which leaves residue on your skin and rings in bathtubs. Few "soap" bar manufacturers use actual soap in their products, hence the marketing euphemism *bath bar*, which is concocted from nonsoap cleaning agents, hardeners, and perfumes.

Most people confuse *detergent* with soap. They are not the same thing. Powdered laundry detergent poured into gasoline will no more dissolve than sand will. Even a true powdered soap simply poured into gas and stirred will not dissolve well. This is because it takes *heated* gasoline to melt soap powders, releasing the hardeners and binding agents used to make the powder. And the heating process is dangerous in the extreme. We're not even going to go into it here.

To safely make a jelled or thickened liquid, you may dissolve a large quantity of crumbled Styrofoam into the gasoline, or make a cold mix paste with cooking lard, stirring it until the lard is well saturated with gas. A gasoline and lard mix looks disgusting, but it works. Liquified animal fat and gasoline will mix if the fat isn't treated with hardeners and binders like it is in soap products. Fat itself is flammable, as anyone who has ever experienced a kitchen grease fire can testify, and with gasoline in it as an accelerant, it's a serious incendiary.

An effective way to deliver Molotovs is to throw a couple of unfused ones aboard a hostile vessel so they'll shatter and spill gas or napalm mix, then light it off with a flare, or fuse the last Molotov.

Emergency Drills

Once you've prepared your vessel and familiarized yourself with all your weapons and equipment, it's time to develop your tactics. Because individual vessels and crews are so different, we can't go into detail here, but the basics are the same for everybody. Practice what you and your crew should do in these scenarios:

1. Emergency Radio Procedures
2. Suspicious Vessel Sighted
3. General Quarters
4. Suspicious Vessel Closing
5. Battle Stations
6. Hostile Vessel In Chase
7. Hostile Vessel Coming Alongside
8. Pirates Boarding
9. Pirates On Board
10. Prisoner Handling
11. Alarm System Alert

1. Emergency Radio Procedures

In trouble, especially if someone is chasing or trying to board you, it's hard to keep a calm and clear voice, but when making an emergency call of any kind, *if you can't be understood you can't be helped.*

Listeners have to know your location and identification, the description of your craft, and your situation. To get all this across in the shortest possible time, you should use the international phonetic alphabet, spelling out what might be misunderstood.

Channel 16 on your VHF marine radio, and now channel 9, are the emergency channels, reserved just for *Mayday, Pan-Pan,* and *Security* calls. They are monitored by the U.S. Coast Guard and some commercial and pleasure vessels. Remember, channels 16 and 9 are *only* for warning and requests for help. Even short conversations are forbidden on these channels.

Mayday calls are only for life threatening situations. *Pan-Pan* calls are for when your vessel or someone on it needs help, but is not in life-or-death trouble. *Security* calls are for navigation and weather hazards, such as if you're underway in heavy fog, or in restricted waterways where others can't see you.

Radio Phonetics Pronunciation Guide

A	Alfa	**AL**	FAH	N	November	NO	**VEM**	BER
B	Bravo	**BRA**	VOH	O	Oscar	**OSS**	KAH	
C	Charlie	HAR	LEE	P	Poppa	PAH	**PAH**	
D	Delta	**DELL**	TAH	Q	Quebec	KEY	**BECK**	
E	Echo	**ECK**	OH	R	Romeo	**ROW**	ME OH	
F	Foxtrot	**FOKS**	TROT	S	Sierra	SEE	**AIR** AH	
G	Golf	GOLF		T	Tango	**TANG**	GO	
H	Hotel	HOH	**TELL**	U	Uniform	YOU	NEEFORM	
I	India	**IN** DEE AH		V	Victor	**VIK**	TAH	
J	Juliet	**JEW** LEE ETT		W	Whiskey	**WISS**	KEY	
K	Kilo	**KEY**	LOW	X	X-Ray	**EX**	RAY	
L	Lima	**LEE**	MA	Y	Yankee	**YANG**	KEY	
M	Mike	MIKE		Z	Zulu	**ZOO**	LOO	

2. Suspicious Vessel Sighted

Only an experienced eye will be able to recognize a suspicious vessel from any other. The tip-offs are subtle, usually something out of place, the dress or actions of the people on board, or the way the craft is being handled.

The procedure of studying vessel types and knowing their construction and performance capabilities should become habitual for you and your crew, so you will know best how to deal with a potential enemy. If you see a suspicious vessel, it's a good idea to photograph it, and write down its description, name, and any identifying markings or numbers, along with the location, and time of sighting.

3. General Quarters

General quarters is the naval warning order to prepare for an emergency. It conveys exactly the right message: *stand by for whatever might happen.*

Sounding general quarters may be done verbally if your craft is small enough, or you could install a horn or bell signal. At the sounding of general quarters, each crew member goes to an assigned place on the vessel, and breaks out protective and emergency equipment, such as body armor vests, life jackets, and gas masks. Whomever is responsible for radio communications stands by the set, ready to transmit.

4. Suspicious Vessel Closing

If a suspicious vessel begins to close on you or if you are approaching it to offer assistance, radio your situation and actions at once to the Coast Guard or another vessel in the area, so someone knows what you're doing and where you are.

Do not automatically tie up alongside or board a vessel that seems to be abandoned, or has people on it requesting assistance.

Radio all the information to the Coast Guard first, and let the people aboard the suspect vessel know you are doing it. Only board once you are reasonably sure of your own safety, take a concealed pistol or knife with you, and have someone on your vessel ready to cover you with a firearm.

5. Battle Stations

Battle stations is one of the most easily understood nautical commands you can give. It is different from general quarters in that battle stations is *the definite order to prepare to fight.*

At the first sign of hostile action, sound battle stations by voice or other signal. The radio operator must immediately send a MAYDAY call. Once battle stations is sounded, those crew assigned to firearms or other weapons will load, move to firing positions, and stand by to shoot. Other crew without weapons stay at their general quarters posts unless they have a different assignment for battle stations.

6. Hostile Vessel In Chase

A hostile vessel is different from a suspicious vessel in that its hostile intentions are confirmed.

If you have a hostile vessel chasing you, continue to send your MAYDAY, and if the vessel is firing at you, or if you can't outrun it and you *know* it means harm, fire tracers across its bow. Such warning shots on your behalf are important, because they signal your intention to fight back, and most pirates will quit right there.

If after your warning shots the hostile vessel continues to pursue or fire on you, then place aimed fire on the vessel to damage or disable it.

7. Hostile Vessel Coming Alongside

If a hostile vessel is trying to grapnel you and tie up alongside, sweep its decks with suppressive fire if the crew is shooting at you, or fire into its engine bay or waterline to hole it if they are not. This is also usually a good opportunity to use flares, smoke, tear gas, and Molotovs to drive off an attacker.

8. Pirates Boarding

If pirates are boarding you, and you've warned them verbally or with shots, then you must deliver volume fire directly at the pirates themselves to save the lives of yourself and your crew and passengers.

Remember, in any self defense situation, you must be able to testify later that *you did not shoot to kill, but to save your life and stop an attacker.*

9. Pirates Aboard

Once pirates get aboard, take advantage of your gas masks. You can pop smoke and tear gas aboard your own vessel to confuse and force boarders over the side. In close range fighting, keep in mind the penetration power of your firearms ammunition and don't fire where it would endanger any of your crew who are taking cover below.

10. Prisoner Handling

Because you've prepared for trouble, you stand an excellent chance of winning a confrontation so decisively you may end up with prisoners and even a captured vessel. Pirates expect easy victims and aren't ready to deal with organized resistance.

Tear gassed or wounded pirates are generally easy to restrain by tying up or handcuffing, and you can tow their vessel and them back to port and the authorities. Of course, you might not want prisoners, because of the legal complications. Disable their vessel and set them adrift, or beach them somewhere and sink their boat.

11. Alarm System Alert

Alarm systems are usually set when you're docked or anchored out somewhere, and an alarm in the middle of the night means trouble indeed. Because the odds are you and your crew will be asleep when this happens, you must have clear and simple procedures to follow.

Again, the differences in each vessel and crew will determine the details of what you plan, but the point is the potential danger of a late night alert is so great that you must assume the worst.

Generally, you should have a firearm and tear gas spray close at hand, and once awake, make the split second decision to give the intruder a warning or to use immediate force.

Daily Security Procedures

Cruises and weekend jaunts have a holiday atmosphere and guard watches or security checks seem unnecessary. Boating magazines aren't much help, either. They promote pleasure and rarely even hint at routine nautical hazards, much less attacks by pirates.

The well being and survival of your passengers and crew is your first responsibility, so you must make security procedures so much a part of your daily routine that they become habits, just like monitoring the weather reports and avoiding collisions. All of the procedures you follow will depend on you, but here's a basic list to incorporate with your other nautical precautions.

Routine inspections of security and protective equipment. Keep your alarm system, night vision devices, and portable radio batteries updated, and your flares, smoke, tear gas, and ammunition fresh, firing off the old lots for training and restocking with new once or twice a year. Check your gas mask filters and air pack bottles frequently. Keep written records of the inspection dates of everything.

Study all vessels encountered in remote places for suspicious signs. Be especially careful of speed boats rapidly and suddenly approaching you, and old, small craft signaling for help. Even well maintained, expensive yachts can be dangerous. Look for people aboard with weapons, people who don't seem to belong on such craft, or signs of damage or disorganization that might indicate the vessel has been taken over by pirates.

Arrange watches at night and in secluded locations. This elementary precaution is not only good for keeping clear of intruders, it works to protect you against accidents, fires, and people overboard.

Regularly scan the areas around you night and day with binoculars and night vision devices. Make this as automatic as breathing. Besides helping to keep anyone from surprising you, it's good nautical practice anytime.

Keep someone constantly posted by radio of your location and destination. In the military, this is called making situation reports, or "sit-reps." Schedule your sit-reps to be given at frequent enough intervals so that if you go missing, it won't be too long before someone notices and comes looking.

Bon Voyage

Sources and References

Here are sellers and manufacturers of the equipment listed in *High Seas Security:*

Silent Partner Body Armor
612 3rd Street
Gretna, LA 70053
(504) 366-4851
Architectural protective materials and Kevlar products

Radio Shack
(Division of Tandy Corp.)
Fort Worth, TX 76102
Security devices and marine communications equipment

Standard Communications
P.O. Box 92151
Los Angeles, CA 90009-2151
(310) 532-5300
Marine communications.

U.S. Cavalry
2855 Centennial Ave.
Radcliff, KY 40160-9000
1-800-333-5102
Body armor, night vision equipment, smoke & tear gas devices.

Other books and manuals related to subjects in *High Seas Security:*

Outlaws of The Ocean
G.O.W. Mueller and Freda Adler
Two criminologists examine piracy, drug smuggling, trading in aliens, boat theft, killing of whales, etc.

Deal The First Deadly Blow! An Encyclopedia of Unarmed and Hand-To-Hand Combat!
Adapted from US Army FM 21-15 (Combatives). A total training source for unarmed and hand-to-hand combat.

The Essential Elements of Personal Combat (With or Without Weapons)
Bradley J. Steiner
This book addresses important aspects of individual close-quarters battle and self-defense.

Modern Ballistic Armor
Duncan Long
Details the myriad uses to which Kevlar cloth may be put.

Index

YOU WILL ALSO WANT TO READ: